W9-BSK-992

Give me your tired, your poor,
your huddled masses yearning to breathe free,
the wretched refuse of your teeming shore.
Send these, the homeless, the tempest-tossed to me,

ARAB AMERICANS

Sharon Cromwell

AMERICAN IMMIGRANTS

Rourke
Publishing LLC
Vero Beach, Florida 32964

www.rourkepublishing.com

PHOTO CREDITS: Ahmad Al Rubaye/AFP: p. 20; George Graham Bain Collection/Library of Congress: p. 23; Bettmann/Corbis: pp. 16, 25; Corbis: p. 6; Department of Defense: p. 18; Chris Fairclough/CFW Images: p. 4; FedEx Kinko's Archive: p. 36; Lewis Wickes Hine/New York Public Library: p. 15; Hulton Archive/Getty Images: p. 38; Ed Kashi/Corbis: p. 28; Library of Congress: pp. 11, 13, 24; NAFF Collection/Archives Center/National Museum of American History/Smithsonian Institution: p. 22; Mike Nelson/AFP: p. 32; Robert Nickelsberg/Getty Images: pp. 29, 41; Kazuyoshi Nomacki/Corbis: pp. 7, 9; Bill Pugliano/Corbis: pp. 27, 30, 42; Paul J. Richards/AFP: p. 34; David Stiuka/Getty Images: p. 35; Len and Libby Traubman: pp. 40, 43; Underwood & Underwood/Library of Congress: p. 24.

Cover picture shows a group of Muslim women in Boston [Andrew Lichtenstein/Corbis].

Produced for Rourke Publishing by Discovery Books
Editor: Gill Humphrey
Designer: Ian Winton
Photo researcher: Rachel Tisdale

Library of Congress Cataloging-in-Publication Data

Cromwell, Sharon, 1947-
  Arab Americans / Sharon Cromwell.
     p. cm. -- (American immigrants)
  Includes bibliographical references.
  Audience: Grades 4-6.
  ISBN 978-1-60044-610-8
  1. Arab Americans--History--Juvenile literature. 2. Arab Americans--Social conditions--Juvenile literature. 3. Immigrants--United States--History--Juvenile literature. 4. Immigrants--United States--Social conditions--Juvenile literature. 5. United States--Emigration and immigration--Juvenile literature. 6. Arab countries--Emigration and immigration--Juvenile literature. I. Title.
  E184.A65C755 2008
  973'.04927--dc22
                              2007020169

TABLE OF CONTENTS

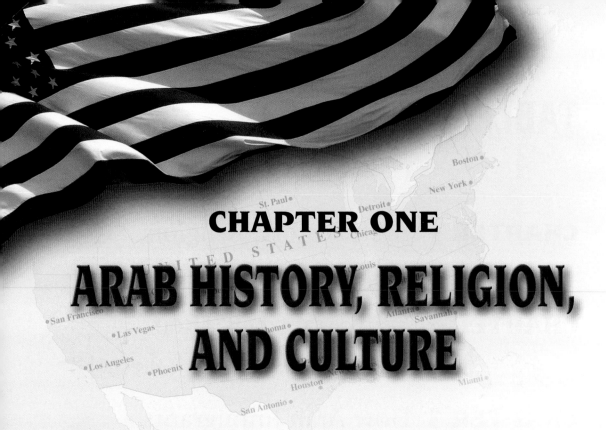

CHAPTER ONE
ARAB HISTORY, RELIGION, AND CULTURE

Today, Arabs live all over the world. Their original **homelands** were countries across North Africa, the **Middle East**, and the **Arabian Peninsula**. Much of this land is desert or scrubland, high mountains, and fertile river valleys and coastal areas.

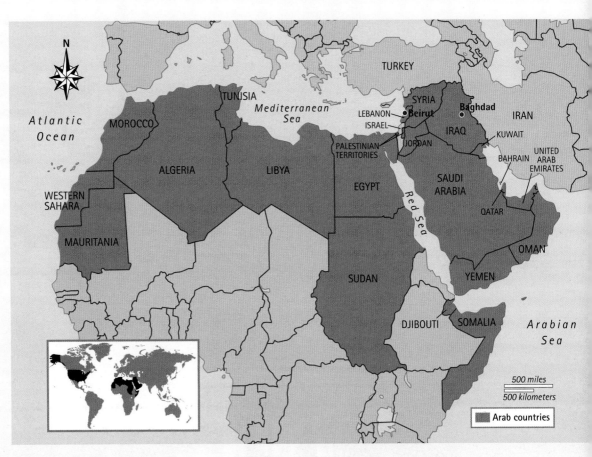

Arabs live in many countries. This map shows the main Arab nations of the world.

Most Arabs are Muslims. They follow the religion of **Islam**. Not all Arabs are Muslims, and not all Muslims see themselves as Arabs. Some Middle Eastern Christians and followers of other religions call themselves Arabs. The Jews, who also live in the Middle East, call themselves Jews and Israelis, not Arabs. Most Arabs speak Arabic. Spoken Arabic has many **dialects** that differ from place to place.

(Opposite) A simple home in a rural area of Morocco. There is no electricity or piped water. Water has to be collected from a well in plastic bottles.

The awesome building of the Dome of the Rock dominates the city of Jerusalem. Although Jerusalem is now under Israeli control, it is a special holy place for Muslims, Jews, and Christians. Only Muslims are allowed to worship at the Dome of the Rock.

Early History of the Arabs

The Arabs are an ancient people. An early Arab civilization settled along the Nile River valley some 6,000 years ago. The people grew crops and **domesticated** animals. Some settled along the Euphrates,

Tigris, and Karun rivers (in modern Iraq and Iran). Other Arabs never settled. They roamed the desert lands with their animals. These people are called **nomads**.

Islam

Muslims believe in the same God as Christians and Jews. They believe that the words in their holy book, the Koran (also spelled Qur'an) come from "Allah" (Arabic for "God"). Muslims believe that

Evening prayers take place outside the Great Mosque in the holy city of Mecca, Saudi Arabia. The city often has to cope with up to 2 million Muslim pilgrims.

the Angel Gabriel spoke these words to the Prophet Muhammad, who lived on the Arabian Peninsula between A.D. 570–632. The religion of Islam is based on the teachings in the Koran.

After Muhammad's death, Arab Muslims from the Arabian Peninsula conquered many lands. These lands stretched from North Africa to Persia (modern Iran) to Europe. They formed a vast Islamic Empire. By 750, Islam had spread across the Arab world and beyond.

MATH AND SCIENCE

The Arabs invented algebra. They were the first to use zero in math. Arab scientists talked of Earth rotating on an axis long before other scientists did.

The Koran

Muslims must try to obey the teachings in the Koran. The most important teachings are called the Five Pillars of Islam:

- to believe in the one God (Allah) and his Prophet Muhammad
- to pray five times a day
- to journey to Mecca (in modern Saudi Arabia) at least once in a lifetime
- to **fast** during the month of **Ramadan**
- to give to charity.

*(Opposite) Arabic **calligraphy** has always been an important part of Islamic art. Here people are embroidering cloth with a bold Arabic design.*

Many Muslims belong to a group called the **Sunnis**. Another group is the **Shia**. Shia wanted Muhammad's family to lead Muslims after Muhammad died. Sunnis wanted his followers to lead. Differences between the two groups have led to conflict, especially in modern Iraq.

Islamic Art

Islamic culture thrived between the eighth and thirteenth centuries. This was called the Golden Age of the Islamic Empire. The people built beautiful **mosques** with arches, domes, and colorful walls. Other arts and crafts grew too, like carpet making and cloth weaving, calligraphy, woodcarving, and making glass and ceramic objects. Soon trading routes were carrying goods to China, the **Byzantine Empire**, India, and Southeast Asia.

AN ISLAMIC CALIPH

A thirteenth-century Chinese writer describes a caliph (leader): "The king wears a turban (headdress) of silk brocade and foreign cotton stuff. On each new moon and full moon he puts on an eight-sided, flat-topped headdress of pure gold, set with the most precious jewels in the world."

The Ottoman Empire

In the sixteenth century, the Ottoman Turks conquered much of the Islamic Empire. They ruled their Arab world from Constantinople (now Istanbul, Turkey), until after World War I (1914-1918). Ottoman rule influenced Islamic art, architecture, and society. During this time, for example, Muslim women could own property and they could not be forced to marry.

By the nineteenth century, the Ottoman Empire was in trouble. The government needed more money. They forced the Arab people to pay more taxes. Many people struggled to feed their families. By the twentieth century Arabs wanted freedom and their own national identity.

This nineteenth-century photograph shows Palestinian villagers working on the land. Life was hard for these people.

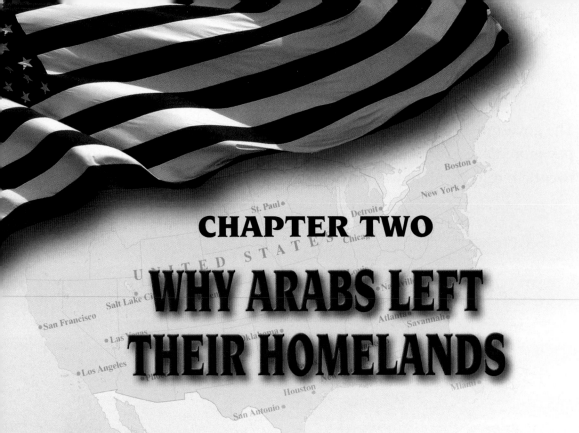

CHAPTER TWO

WHY ARABS LEFT THEIR HOMELANDS

People leave their homelands for many reasons. These include war, poverty, famine, too few jobs, and a lack of freedom. People from Arab countries have suffered from all these problems over the last 150 years. Thousands left their homelands and many came to the United States. They came in three waves of immigration.

The First Wave

In 1876, the Centennial Exhibition marked 100 years of American independence. It took place in Philadelphia, Pennsylvania. Merchants from around the world brought their goods. Arabs and Turks sent 1,600 people and businesses. They sold everything from coffee to **rosaries** carved in Jerusalem.

Some Arabs who visited the exhibition stayed in the United States. Other traders carried news of American wealth to their homelands. In both ways, the exhibition helped start the first wave of Arab immigration.

The people who came to the United States in the first wave were mostly Syrian, Lebanese, or Palestinian. Many were young, uneducated

The 1876 Centennial Exhibition. This photograph shows part of the Egyptian section.

AN UNCOMFORTABLE JOURNEY

At first, a boat was the only way for **immigrants** to reach the United States. George Hamid came to the United States when he was ten years old. He describes the voyage:

"Our quarters were cramped beyond imagination. The odor, heavy and ever-present, made us sick at first....The food was the world's worst. The filth was knee-deep...."

These young girls are working in one of Syria's largest silk factories at the beginning of the twentieth century. They are taking care of boiling the silkworm cocoons.

men who had been struggling farmers. Farming had become harder as insect plagues ruined crop after crop. Other immigrants had been farming and selling silk. This industry was also in trouble. Silkworm disease had hurt production and cheaper silk was being produced in Eastern Asia.

Many immigrant men left behind families. They hoped to send money home once they had jobs. Some dreamed of returning home with great fortunes. The first wave began around 1880 and ended in 1924. That year, a new law limited Arab immigration.

Getting to the United States was expensive and unpleasant. Immigrants needed money for the trip. Then they needed money to survive until they found work.

Although the first Arab immigrants were men, some wives did make their way to the U.S. to join their husbands. This Arab woman was photographed at Ellis Island by the famous photographer L.W. Hine in 1926.

Palestinian women and children carrying their possessions along a dusty road. They have been forced to leave their homes after the conflict that led to the creation of Israel in 1948. Some of these refugees made their way to the United States.

Most immigrants entered the country through Ellis Island in New York City. They spent hours in long lines before getting into the country. Some failed the medical test and were sent home. U.S.

border guards rarely spoke Arabic and so they recorded immigrants' names in English. This often changed both the spelling and sound of the name.

The Second Wave

The second wave of Arab immigrants arrived between 1948 and 1966. In 1948, after a war in the Middle East, Israel became a country. It was created from lands claimed by Palestinians. Many Palestinians fled from their homes. They became **refugees**. Thousands of Palestinians **emigrated** to the United States. By this time, travel to the U.S. was quicker. Many immigrants arrived by plane.

Rich immigrants from Egypt and Iraq emigrated to the United States in the 1950s because new governments had taken over their countries. These governments took their land and money.

In the second wave, over half of Arab immigrants were Muslims. They were better educated and had more money than earlier immigrants.

AN ARAB-AMERICAN VIEW

Naomi Shihab Nye is a Palestinian Arab-American writer. In one essay, she wrote: "Each time I returned to the **West Bank** as an adult, I had experiences that made me grit my teeth....Luckily, I met many Jews over the years...who had a deeper concept of what the Jewish-Arab relationship could and should have been—cousins, from the start."

The Third Wave

The Middle East and North Africa have suffered violence since 1967. Tens of thousands of Arabs have lost their homes, lands, and businesses. Friends and family members have been killed. Arabs caught in the fighting began seeking safer places to live. This pushed thousands of people into leaving their own countries.

Part of Beirut, the capital city of Lebanon, is devastated by the civil war of 1975-1991. The conflict lasted 26 years and led many people to emigrate to the United States.

Fighting and violence included:

• 1967: Israel defeated Egypt, Syria, and Jordan in the Six-Day War. Israel's strength worried many Arabs. Some emigrated to the United States.

- 1973: Egypt and Syria attacked Israel. They tried to take back some of the land lost in 1967.
- 1975 to 1991: **Civil war** raged in Lebanon. People died, homes were destroyed, and the capital, Beirut, was badly damaged. About 90,000 people left Lebanon between 1965 and 1992.
- 1981 to 1988: Arabs fled Iraq to escape the Iran-Iraq War.
- 1987: Palestinians fought against the Israeli government. This was called the Intifada. It lasted more than five years. Many Palestinians fled to the United States.
- 1990s: Many Iraqis left their homeland. They tried to escape the harsh rule of the **dictator** Saddam Hussein. At the same time, Arabs were leaving Egypt and Syria because they had few freedoms and few job opportunities.
- 2003: The United States and **allies** invaded Iraq. They wanted to remove Saddam Hussein and find **weapons of mass destruction**. U.S. troops soon found themselves occupying a country torn by fighting between Shia and Sunni Muslims. The situation is leading Iraq toward civil war.

In 1965, the U.S. government had relaxed immigration laws. From then until 1992, the number of Arabs emigrating to the United States increased. The third wave of immigrants was three times larger than the first wave. Many of these Arabs were Palestinian. Some immigrants from this wave were skilled workers or well educated. Others were students eager for the opportunities in the United States. Today's Palestinian-American population is between 50,000 and 200,000.

Baghdad, August 2006. Some Iraqi men looking at the wreckage of a car after a bomb and missile attack. More and more people want to leave Iraq to escape the conflict that is threatening their lives.

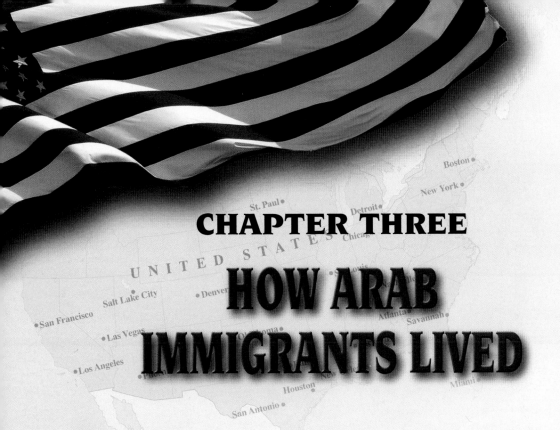

CHAPTER THREE
HOW ARAB IMMIGRANTS LIVED

By 1900, many Syrian immigrants had settled in New York City. A lively neighborhood on Washington Street was known as "Little Syria" because so many Syrian Americans lived there. Here they gathered and talked in coffee houses. Some wore colorful traditional dress. In the stores, they could buy Arab foods. Many worked in the local Syrian-owned textile stores and silk factories.

PEDDLING

Many early Arab Americans worked as peddlers. A peddler bought goods in Little Syria and sold them from his pack. Peddlers sold cloth, jewelry, and many other items. In the early twentieth century, catalog companies such as Sears, Roebuck began mail order businesses. Local department stores opened. Peddling slowly disappeared.

This peddler was successful enough to own a carriage. Other peddlers had to carry their goods in packs on their backs. These packs sometimes weighed up to 200 pounds.

Later, wealthier Christian Arab Americans moved to Brooklyn. They founded a bank, churches, newspapers, and political clubs. In 1907, the Syrian Ladies' Aid Society was established. The society helped Syrian women who had just arrived in the United States.

Earning a Living

Arab immigrants were sometimes treated unfairly by other Americans. This made it hard for them to earn a living. So, many Arabs settled and worked in Arab communities. By 1910, many Arab Americans could speak and write English. They opened their own businesses making silk, other materials, and clothing. In 1924, Syrian immigrants had twenty-five silk factories in New Jersey.

This early twentieth-century photograph shows a beverage vendor in the Syrian quarter of New York City. The vendor is wearing a fez – a traditional Arab hat. The young man who has just had a drink is carrying a newspaper written in Arabic.

These immigrants are being taught English in a class given by the Ford Motor Company where many of them worked. Some of these men would have emigrated from Arab countries. The photograph was taken at the beginning of the twentieth century.

WORKING IN THE MILL

Hannah Sabbagh Shakir emigrated from Lebanon. At 14, she worked in a textile mill in Massachusetts:

"I learned how to operate the looms...just like a man...some days the machines would keep breaking down, the threads would keep snapping, and you had to undo the damaged sections. Other days everything went smoothly."

From around 1914, many Muslim Arab immigrants settled in Detroit and Dearborn, Michigan. There, they worked for the car companies. They also settled around Pittsburgh, Pennsylvania, working in the steel mills.

In Michigan City, Indiana, Syrian Muslims worked in factories building Pullman train cars. There were so many Arab workers that one factory closed for 'Id al-Fitr (also called Eid-ul-Fitr). This day of

A photograph showing the inside of a Syrian store on Washington Street in New York City in 1919. The customers and store owner are wearing western-style clothes. These customers have come to buy marcouck, which is traditional Syrian flat bread.

feasting, giving, and prayers marks the end of Ramadan. Many of the Muslim workers took time off for prayers and celebrations.

Fitting into Society

First-wave Arab immigrants had mixed feelings about American life. American values and culture often seemed strange. In traditional Arab families men were the head of the household. Women were obedient and usually stayed home to care for the children. Parents and religious leaders arranged young people's marriages. Living in the United States changed Arab lifestyles. For example, young people began to ask to choose their own marriage partners.

Between World War I and II, second-**generation** Arab Americans played down their Arab roots. They wanted to fit in. Most still celebrated their Arab culture through their religions at churches or mosques. Arabs also joined Arab-American organizations.

JOSEPH J. JACOBS, ARAB-AMERICAN INDUSTRIALIST

Joseph J. Jacobs was born in 1916 to Lebanese parents. He grew up in Brooklyn and started an engineering and construction company. He wrote:

"Our families wanted us to be Americans, but not at the expense of our own heritage....Most of the **ethnic** immigrants, the Italians, Poles, Germans, Scandinavians, and others tended to live in [separate communities] where the mother tongue was the everyday language and English was kept primarily for commerce with Americans. So did the Lebanese."

The Islamic Center of America Mosque, Detroit, Michigan. This impressive mosque is one of the largest in the U.S.

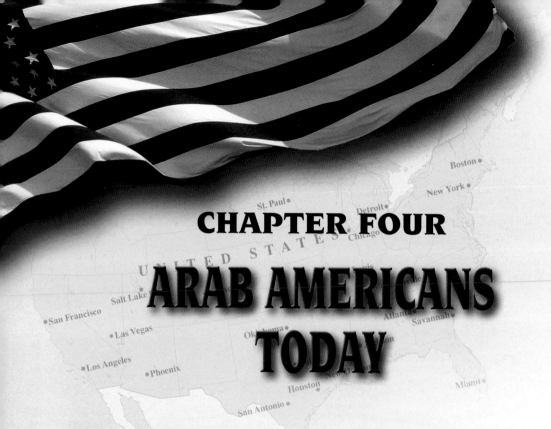

CHAPTER FOUR
ARAB AMERICANS TODAY

A rab Americans live in many different kinds of communities. But most live in cities with other Arabs. Large Arab-American populations are found in California, New York, and Michigan.

Muslim children are reciting a prayer during Ramadan at the Islamic Institute of Knowledge in Dearborn, Michigan.

About 340,000 Arab Americans live in Los Angeles, California. The climate and landscape there reminded immigrants of their homelands.

The more-recent immigrants are educated. Many speak English as well as Arabic. It has been easier for them to find work. They work as doctors, lawyers, and engineers. Others work in the computer industry or have started their own businesses.

Arab American women on a street in New York City, May 2005. Linda Sarsour (first person on the left) works for the Arab American Association in New York City. This organization offers advice to the 300,000 Arab Americans living in the area.

ARAB-AMERICAN WOMEN

Many Arab-American women **descended** from first-wave Arab immigrants have little to do with traditional Arab culture. They act and dress like other American women. But some women still live in traditional communities. They enjoy fewer freedoms and opportunities. They wear head coverings and simple clothing to honor their religion and culture.

Muslim Arab-Americans' lives generally center around the mosque. The mosque is a place of worship and also a place for community activities, such as weddings and funerals. There are

Volunteers taking part in the Yalla Vote Walk, in October 2004, in Dearborn, Michigan. The walk was sponsored by the Arab American Institute. It wanted to remind Arab Americans to vote in the November elections.

between 1,400 and 3,000 mosques, prayer centers, and Islamic centers in America today.

Some Muslims think American culture—including rock music, television shows, and fashions—will drive their children away from their religion.

Arabs who emigrated to the United States after World War II were more involved in politics than earlier immigrants. Many disagree with U.S. actions in the Middle East and the U.S. government's support for Israel in its fight with some Middle East Arab countries. This support has angered Muslims around the world.

THE ARAB AMERICAN NATIONAL MUSEUM

The Arab American National Museum is in Dearborn, Michigan. It opened in 2005. Its purpose is to tell the story of Arab immigration and...

"...to document, preserve, celebrate, and educate the public on the history, life, culture, and contributions of Arab Americans."

September 11, 2001

On September 11, 2001, Arab **terrorists** flew two airplanes into the World Trade Center in New York City. They destroyed both buildings. Another plane was flown into the Pentagon near Washington, D.C. Passengers on board a fourth aircraft fought the terrorists. They crashed in Pennsylvania. About 3,000 people were killed during these attacks.

The terrorists were not American Muslims. They were from the terrorist group **al Qaeda**. Still, Arab Americans feared some Americans would blame all Arab and Muslim Americans for the attacks. Since September 11, some Arab Americans have been treated unfairly. Others have been victims of violence.

A sign showing sympathy for the victims of the September 11 attacks is hung outside the King Fahd Mosque in Culver City, California.

PRESIDENT BUSH SPEAKS

President George W. Bush met with Muslim leaders on September 17, 2001. He spoke against anti-Muslim feelings.

"Like the good folks standing with me, the American people were... outraged at last Tuesday's attacks [on September 11, 2001]. And so were Muslims all across the world....The face of terror is not the true faith of Islam...."

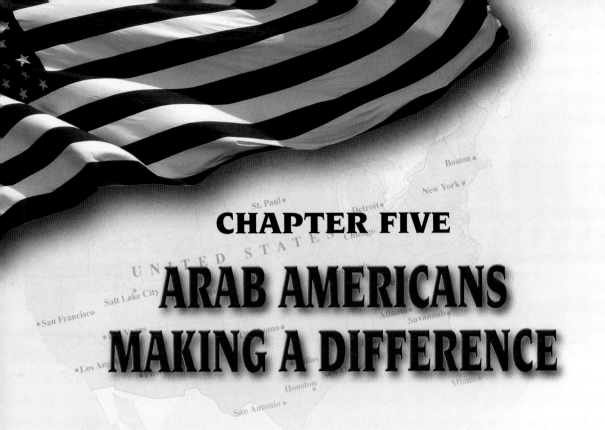

CHAPTER FIVE

ARAB AMERICANS MAKING A DIFFERENCE

Arab Americans have faced many problems. Still, they are a successful immigrant group. Many are hard working and skilful in business. They have opened stores, factories, and restaurants. Others have successful careers in medicine, science, finance, banking, and law. They have influenced many areas of American life.

POPULAR ARAB FOODS

Arab foods are popular in America today. These include hummus (a chickpea puree), tabbouleh (a cracked wheat salad), pita bread, and shish kebabs (meat on sticks). Both cities and smaller communities have Arab-American restaurants.

Entertainment and Sport

Arab Americans have given much to the entertainment industry. Danny Thomas (1912–1991) was a talented comedian and television

The Lebanese-American comedian and actress Kathy Najimy made people laugh in the long running Kathy and Mo Show. *In 2004, she was named "Woman of the Year" by Ms. Magazine.*

star. He was the founder of St. Jude Children's Research Hospital in Memphis, Tennessee. Other well-known actors of Arab descent include F. Murray Abraham (the film *Amadeus*), Jamie Farr (*M*A*S*H*), Kathy Najimy (*Veronica's Closet*), and Tony Shalhoub (*Monk*). Marlo Thomas, daughter of Danny Thomas (*That Girl*) also writes books.

Arab Americans also have made contributions to sports. Bill George (1929–1982), played **professional** football for the Chicago Bears. He was elected to the Pro Football Hall of Fame in 1974.

Doug Flutie, quarterback for the New England Patriots prepares to hand the ball off against the Green Bay Packers during a game in 2005.

Doug Flutie (1962–), the football quarterback, won the Heisman Trophy. He later played in the United States Football League, Canadian Football League, and the National Football League.

Business and Politics

Arab Americans are skilful business people. Paul Orfalea (1947–), a Lebanese American, founded Kinko's. This is a chain of business service stores. The first Kinko's opened near a California university. Today, more than 1,200 stores exist worldwide. In 2000, Orfalea started the Orfalea Family Foundation. This foundation provides educational programs for children with disabilities and underprivileged young people.

Arab Americans have also played a role in U.S. politics. Ralph Nader (1934–), is of Lebanese descent. He has worked hard to protect consumer rights and the environment. In 2002, John E. Sununu (1964–) became the youngest member of the U.S. Senate. He is of Irish and Palestinian-Lebanese descent. His father, John H. Sununu is the former Governor of New Hampshire, and former White House Chief of Staff under President George H. W. Bush.

Donna Shalala (1941–) became president of the University of Miami in 2001. She is a Lebanese American. She was Secretary of Health and Human Services for President Bill Clinton. Shalala served from 1993–2001, the longest serving Secretary of Health in U.S. History.

(Opposite) Paul Orfalea, the successful businessman,
inside one of his Kinko's stores in 1995.

Literature and Music

Kahlil (Khalil) Gibran (1883–1931), is a famous Arab-American writer. He came to the United States from Lebanon in 1893. His book, *The Prophet*, was written in 1923. It is still read today. Ameen Rihani (Amin al-Rihani) (1876–1940) is called the "founding father of Arab-American literature." He was the first Arab American to write in English. Arab-American writers and poets today include Naomi Shihab Nye, Diana Abu-Jaber, and Lisa Suhair.

Arab Americans have changed music. Frank Zappa (1940–1993) blended rock, classical, and other types of music. Paula Abdul had many hit songs in the 1980s and 1990s. World music is now popular. Non-Arab Americans are listening to Arabic-style music. Some music blends Arabic sounds with funk and hip-hop.

Rock guitarist and composer Frank Zappa with his son Dweezil in 1985. He wrote and recorded hundreds of pieces of music during his musical career.

CHAPTER SIX
THE FUTURE

Between 1990 and 2000, an estimated 328,712 Arabs emigrated to the United States. Most of them were Muslims. Many came from Egypt. These immigrants hoped for better jobs and more political freedom.

Today, the majority of Arab Americans are U.S. citizens. Most were born in the United States. Less than half were born elsewhere and became citizens after immigrating here.

Arab Americans have not always been treated fairly in the United States. Some people do not trust Muslims, especially those born in

A REASON FOR HOPE

In the 1990s, Len and Libby Traubman started a discussion group. They brought together local Jewish and Palestinian Americans to discuss how they felt about problems in the Middle East. In 2003, they held the first Peace Camp. In 2006, 250 Jews, Muslims, and Christians met at Camp Tawonga in California. The goal was for everyone to try to understand each other.

A photograph taken at the 2006 Peace Camp in California. A young Jewish American man (left) talks with a couple of Palestinians from Nablus, a large city controlled by the Palestinian Authority in the West Bank.

other countries. This has made living in the United States more difficult for this immigrant group. Distrust of Arab Americans, especially Muslims, rose after the September 11 attacks. Then, Arab and Muslim Americans were looked at suspiciously at airports, borders, universities, and at work. This is called profiling. It means someone is suspected of a crime based on ethnic background or religion.

Immigration in the Future

The flow of Arab immigration depends partly on what happens in the Arab world and in the United States. In some Arab countries, conflict continues. There, emigration rates will probably rise.

Linda Sarsour talks to an F.B.I. agent about the problems Arab Americans have faced from government agencies since the September 11 attacks. Many people at the meeting complained about the harassment, racial profiling, and **deportations** *that have taken place against their community.*

Recent events have affected some Americans' feelings toward Arabs. Deaths in Israel caused by Palestinian suicide bombers, the events of September 11, 2001, and the war in Iraq have made some people fear and distrust Arab Americans.

Other events make Arab Americans unhappy with their government. Most Arab Americans disagree with the government's support for Israel against the Arabs. They don't like Israel's control of land claimed by the Palestinians and were angry with Israel when it attacked Lebanon in 2006. Problems between Arab Americans and non-Arab Americans will probably continue as long as the United States is involved in Middle Eastern conflicts.

Dearborn, Michigan, August 2006. Hundreds of Arab Americans showing their anger at the Israeli action in Lebanon, which led to the death of innocent Lebanese civilians.

Organizers and speakers in front of a banner at the 2006 Peace Camp. Stopping conflict in the Arab world, and especially in the Middle East, is key to creating better relations between Arab Americans and non-Arab Americans in the United States.

PEACE CAMP EXPERIENCES

Isaac Zones, a young Jewish American, attended a peace camp. He said,

"More than anything else I made personal relationships with Arabs—which I had never done before."

"Once people meet and engage in a safe place, change begins," said Len Traubman.

GLOSSARY

allies (AL ize) — friendly countries that sometimes give military support

al Qaeda (AL KI ee da) — a terrorist organization started in the 1980s by Osama bin Laden and Muhammad Atef. The organization trains terrorists.

Arabian Peninsula (A ruh bi an puh NIN suh luh) — peninsula in southwest Asia bordered by the Red Sea to the west, the Indian Ocean to the south, the Persian Gulf to the east, and the Syrian Desert to the north

Byzantine Empire (BIZ uhn teen EM pire) — empire that existed in southeast Europe and southwest Asia from A.D. 395-1453

calligraphy (kuh LIG ruh fee) — beautiful handwriting, often very decorative

civil war (SIV il wor) — war between different groups, inside the same country

deportations (di por TAY shuhnz) — the forced removal of people from a country

descended (di SEN did) — coming from a family or ethnic group

dialect (DYE uh lekt) — form of a language spoken in a region of a country

dictator (DIK tay tur) — a ruler who has complete power over his or her people

domesticate (duh MESS tik ate) — to tame and raise animals for human use

emigrate (EM uh grate) — to leave one's own country for another; in the new country, that person is an immigrant

ethnic (ETH nik) — having the same cultural background, with the same history and customs

fast (fast) — to go without food

generation (jen uh RAY shuhn) — group of people that make a single step in a line of descent from an ancestor

homeland (home land) — country or area set aside as the home for people of a particular national, cultural, or racial origin

immigrant (IM uh gruhnt) — person who has moved to another country to start a new life

Islam (ISS luhm) — one of the world's major religions. Islam was founded by the Prophet Muhammad in the seventh century.

Middle East (MID uhl eest) — name for the region taken to include these fifteen countries: Libya, Egypt, Israel, Lebanon, Syria, Jordan, Iraq, and Iran; and the Arabian Peninsula countries of Bahrain, Kuwait, Saudi Arabia, United Arab Emirates, Oman, Yemen, and Qatar. It also includes the Palestinian territories — the West Bank and the Gaza Strip.

mosque (mosk) — an Islamic place of worship

nomad (NOH mad) — a person who travels from area to area in search of food and pasture for his or her animals. Some nomads still live in Arab countries today.

Ramadan (RAHM i dahn) — Muslim holy month

refugees (ref yuh JEEZ) — people who are forced to leave their homes because of war or persecution

rosary (ROZE ar ee) — string of beads used in the Catholic church for religious practice

Shia (SHEE a) — one of two major groups within Islam. Shia Muslims share similar beliefs and practices with the Sunni Muslim group. They do not agree on leadership. Most Shia live in the non-Arab countries of Iran and Pakistan. Others live in Lebanon and Iraq.

Sunni (SUHN ee) — one of two major groups within Islam. Sunni Muslims share similar beliefs and practices with the Shia Muslim group. They do not agree on leadership.

terrorist (TER ur ist) — person who uses violence to try to bring about change

weapons of mass destruction (WEP uhns ov mass di STRUHK shuhn) — weapons like nuclear bombs or poisonous gas that can kill thousands of people very quickly

West Bank (west bangk) — area of conflict west of the Jordan River, which some Iraeli's believe is part of Israel, but is inhabited mainly by Palestinians

FURTHER INFORMATION

Places to Visit or Write

Arab American National Museum

13624 Michigan Avenue,

Dearborn,

MI 48126

Tel: (313) 582-AANM, Fax: (313) 582-1086.

Books

Arab Americans. Marilyn D. Anderson. Milwaukee, World Almanac
   Library, 2007.

19 Varieties of Gazelle: Poems of the Middle East. Naomi Shihab Nye.
   Harper Tempest, Greenwillow, 2005.

The Arab Americans. Jean Brodsky Schur. Lucent Books, 2004.

Grandma Hekmatt Remembers: An Arab-American Family Story. Ann
   Morris. Brookfield, Millbrook Press, 2003.

The Arab Americans. Bob Temple. Mason Crest Publishers, 2002.

Websites to Visit

http://www.cair-net.org/default.asp?Page=aboutIslam

The Council on American-Islamic Relations, CAIR. About Islam and American Muslims.

http//traubman.igc.org/camps.htm

More information about Peace Camps.

http://www.religioustolerance.org/islam.htm

Religious Tolerance. Information about Islam.

Video

Bridges Between Cultures. Filmed by Dan Cahill. November 2001. To obtain, contact Dan Cahill at cahilld@nyc.rr.com

DVD

Muhammad: Legacy of a Prophet. Created and produced by Alexander Kronemer and Michael Wolfe. Kikim Media, 2002

INDEX